W9-CUP-944

Cam Newton

By Jon M. Fishman

AMAZING ATHLETES

Lerner Publications ◆ Minneapolis

Lerner Publications Company
A division of Lerner Publishing Group, Inc.
241 First Avenue North
Minneapolis, MN 55401 USA

For reading levels and more information, look up this title at www.lernerbooks.com.

Library of Congress Cataloging-in-Publication Data

Names: Fishman, Jon M., author.
Title: Cam Newton / by Jon M. Fishman.
Description: Minneapolis : Lerner Publications, [2017] | Includes bibliographical references and index.
Identifiers: LCCN 2016010149 (print) | LCCN 2016012517 (ebook) | ISBN 9781512429077 (lb : alk. paper) | ISBN 9781512429084 (pb : alk. paper) | ISBN 9781512429091 (eb pdf)
Subjects: LCSH: Newton, Cam, 1989– | Football players—United States—Biography. | Quarterbacks (Football)—United States—Biography.
Classification: LCC GV939.N42 F57 2017 (print) | LCC GV939.N42 (ebook) | DDC 796.332092—dc23

LC record available at http://lccn.loc.gov/2016010149

Manufactured in the United States of America
1-41567-23392-3/24/2016

TABLE OF CONTENTS

Cam Newton of the Carolina Panthers runs with the ball against the Denver Broncos.

SUPER BOWL 50

With cameras flashing and fans cheering, Carolina Panthers **quarterback** Cam Newton ran onto the field. It was February 7, 2016, and Super Bowl 50 was about to begin. If Cam and his teammates could beat the Denver

Broncos, they would be National Football League (NFL) champions.

Cam had wanted to play in the Super Bowl for most of his life. "I have been dreaming of this moment since I was seven years old," he said. It is the biggest football game of the year.

The Carolina Panthers played the Denver Broncos at Levi's Stadium in Santa Clara, California.

Denver Broncos players chase Cam *(left)* during Super Bowl 50.

With more than 100 million viewers, Super Bowl 50 was one of the most watched TV shows ever.

The game started poorly for the Panthers. Cam couldn't find an open **wide receiver**, and his team made mistakes. The Denver **defense** swarmed to the ball. On **offense**, Broncos quarterback Peyton Manning moved his team down the field. They were ahead at halftime, 13–7.

The second half didn't start out much better for Carolina. Cam still couldn't find open receivers to throw the ball to. Both teams kicked **field goals**. Denver had the lead, 16–10.

Denver's Von Miller *(left)* knocks the ball from Cam's hands.

With time running out on the game clock, it didn't look good for the Panthers.

With about four minutes left in the game, Carolina had the ball. Cam took the **snap** and stepped back. He looked down the field for a wide receiver. As usual, no one was open. He finally spotted someone, but it was too late. As Cam got ready to throw, the ball was swatted out of his hand. Denver players jumped on the ball. Cam watched from his knees as the Broncos celebrated.

Cam Newton kneels on the field after losing the ball.

Denver won the Super Bowl, 24–10. It was a crushing loss for the Panthers. But Cam has proven to be a special player in his short time in the NFL. With their big quarterback calling the plays, Carolina has a bright future.

Cam plays sports video games and watches movies in his spare time. His favorite actor is Denzel Washington.

Cam grew up near Atlanta, Georgia.

BIG BOY

Cameron Jerrell Newton was born on May 11, 1989, in Atlanta, Georgia. Everyone called him Cam. He was a big, athletic kid. Growing up in College Park, Georgia, he loved to play sports with his friends.

Cam especially liked football. He usually played **linebacker**, a position on defense. Other times he played with the offense. The quarterback would hand the ball to Cam and watch him charge through the other team. "He was bigger than all the other kids so no one could tackle him," said childhood friend Morgan Burnett.

Baseball also took up some of Cam's free time.

Cam's childhood friend Morgan Burnett also plays in the NFL. He is a **safety** for the Green Bay Packers.

Morgan Burnett warms up before a game against the Detroit Lions.

But when he was 14 years old, he quit the sport. He didn't like how fast the ball whizzed by him when he was in the **batter's box**. Football was a rough sport, but it didn't hurt as much as getting hit by a baseball.

To fill the time he had been spending on baseball, Cam took up basketball. On the football field, his size and strength were big advantages. But on the basketball court, knocking other players to the ground is a **foul**. "I had to understand the difference between basketball and football, but it was challenging being so big," he said.

When he wasn't playing sports, Cam's family made sure he stayed out of trouble. His mother, Jackie, kept a close eye on his report cards. Cecil, Cam's father, kept the boy busy practicing his football skills and doing odd jobs

Cam *(center)* stands with family and friends in 2011.

to earn money. Cecil made sure that Cam and his brothers, Cecil Jr. and Caylin, worked hard no matter what they were doing.

In 2003, Cam enrolled as a freshman at Westlake High School in Atlanta. His size and skills earned him a place on the **varsity** team. His older brother, Cecil Jr., was the team's **center**.

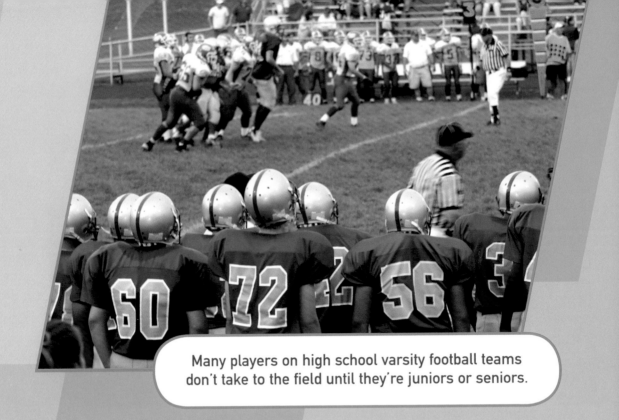

Many players on high school varsity football teams don't take to the field until they're juniors or seniors.

QUARTERBACK ON THE RISE

Cam's strong arm and smart plays on the field had earned him the role of quarterback. But as a freshman, he wasn't expected to play in any games. That changed when Westlake's starting quarterback was injured during a big game.

With television cameras rolling and the stands full of fans, Cam entered a high school varsity game for the first time. He was nervous, but Cecil Jr. was there to help keep him calm. Cam led the team down the field. With just a few yards to go for a touchdown, he tried to take the snap from his brother. But Cam couldn't hold onto the ball. It bounced away, and the other team took possession of the ball. Westlake lost by one point. After the game, Cecil Jr. took the blame for the mistake.

Cam and Cecil Jr.'s little brother Caylin also plays football. He is one of the top-ranked high school players in Georgia.

It didn't take long for Cam to feel more comfortable as Westlake's quarterback. Over the next few years, he caught the attention of **scouts** all around the country. He launched balls far down the field with his powerful right arm. He made good decisions under pressure. He also ran like a **running back**. His talent for throwing and running had college scouts practically drooling.

Cam couldn't wait to play college football. In his last year of high school in 2006, he took classes during the summer. He also took classes online. The extra work allowed him to graduate early from Westlake. In January 2007, Cam began school at the University of Florida. His first day at the school, the football team won the national championship!

Even though he didn't get to play in the game, Cam was happy his new school had won the championship. He had wanted to play big-time college football, and it didn't get bigger than the Florida Gators. But playing for the Gators put a lot of pressure on Cam. Quarterback is the most important position on a football team. Florida coaches and fans would expect him to perform at a high level. Mistakes like losing the ball in important moments couldn't happen.

Cam runs the ball as quarterback for the Florida Gators.

Tim Tebow and Cam celebrate on the sidelines during a Florida Gators game.

FRESH STARTS

In 2007, Tim Tebow was on his way to a monster season as Florida's starting quarterback. That meant Cam spent most of his time on the bench. He finished the season with just 40 yards passing and 103 yards rushing.

The next season, Cam was hopeful he'd earn more playing time. In the first game, he rushed for 10 yards and completed a 14-yard pass. He also injured his ankle. Florida's coaches decided to make Cam a **medical redshirt**. That meant he wouldn't play again in 2008.

Cam didn't react well to the change. He was unhappy that his college career had not gone as planned. Without football to keep him occupied, he got into trouble. In November, Cam was accused of stealing a computer from another Florida student. He was suspended from the football team. Less than two months later, he announced he was leaving Florida.

> Tim Tebow won the **Heisman Trophy** in 2007. He played in the NFL but lasted only three seasons.

Cam needed to start over. He got the chance at Blinn College in Brenham, Texas. Blinn is a **junior college**. That means their football games aren't shown on national TV. It was a more relaxed place to play than Florida had been.

Cam runs toward the end zone to score a touchdown for the Blinn College Buccaneers.

Most of the people Cam knew at Blinn lived nearby in Texas. "During the summer or weekends, everyone would go home," Cam said. "I'd be the only one there, and it was a ghost town. That's when I would think about what I really wanted to do with my life."

Cam knew he could be a football star. He thought about the lessons he'd learned from his parents. He pushed himself to get better.

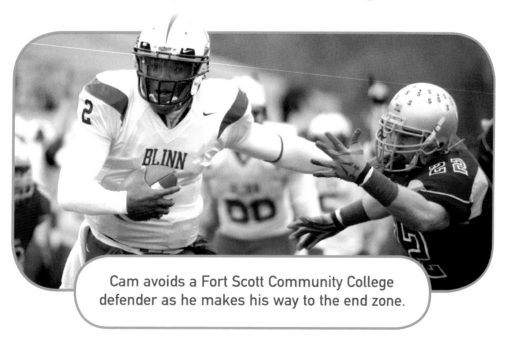

Cam avoids a Fort Scott Community College defender as he makes his way to the end zone.

In 2009, he threw 22 touchdown passes and ran for 17 touchdowns. He helped Blinn win the junior college national championship.

The next year, Cam felt he was ready for **Division I** football again. He joined Auburn University and had an incredible season. He threw

Cam runs the ball for the Auburn University Tigers.

30 touchdown passes and rushed for 20 more.

He led Auburn to the national championship and won the Heisman Trophy!

Cam Newton holds the Heisman Trophy in 2010 in New York City.

Cam poses with NFL chief Roger Goodell after being selected as the first pick overall by the Carolina Panthers in the first round of the NFL draft.

SUPERCAM

Cam's problems at Florida were completely behind him. After the 2010 season, he was widely thought of as the best college player in the country. The Carolina Panthers coaches agreed. They chose Cam with the first pick in the 2011 NFL **Draft**.

Not everyone was convinced Cam would succeed in the NFL. The players are bigger and stronger. Quarterbacks who run a lot, like Cam, take big hits. They often get injured.

In 2011, Cam's strength, size, and speed kept him one step ahead of defenders. He was named Rookie of the Year. Over the next few seasons, he became an NFL superstar. He wowed fans with his running and throwing skills. No quarterback could do both as well as Cam.

Cam looks for a Carolina teammate to throw to during a game against the Cincinnati Bengals.

The big quarterback also does good things off the field. The Cam Newton Foundation supports the needs of young people. The group holds athletic and educational events. It also raises a lot of money for charity. Since his time

Cam spends quality time with Braylon Beam, who served as Honorary Head Coach of the Panthers for a day through the Make-A-Wish Foundation.

in college, Cam has visited elementary schools. As one of the NFL's biggest stars, he has a chance to inspire young fans. Cam talks about working hard and making the most of second chances. He's always willing to spend time with kids and take selfies with them.

In 2015, Cam had his best year yet. In the final game of the season, he threw two touchdown passes and ran for two touchdowns. It was the 31st time he'd scored a rushing touchdown and a passing touchdown in

After the 2015 season, Cam was named NFL Most Valuable Player (MVP).

the same game. That tied the all-time record set by Steve Young. It had taken Young 15 years to set the record, but Cam tied it in just five!

Cam signs autographs and talks with fans in 2011.

Just before the 2016 Super Bowl, Denver quarterback Peyton Manning talked about Cam. Peyton said Cam would be the biggest star in the NFL for the next eight to 10 years. The league is in good hands with Cam leading the way.

Selected Career Highlights

2016 Led the Panthers to Super Bowl 50

2015 Named NFL MVP
Voted to the NFL Pro Bowl for the third time
Led the Panthers to a 15–1 record

2013 Voted to the NFL Pro Bowl for the second time

2011 Voted Offensive Rookie of the Year
Voted to the NFL Pro Bowl for the first time
Chosen with the first overall pick in the NFL draft
Led Auburn to the Division I national championship

2010 Won the Heisman Trophy
Enrolled at Auburn after one year at Blinn

2009 Led Blinn to the junior college national championship
Enrolled at Blinn after two years at Florida

2008 Left Florida after being accused of theft
Sat out the season as a medical redshirt

2007 Spent most of the season on the bench behind starting quarterback Tim Tebow
Enrolled at Florida after high school

Glossary

batter's box: in baseball, the area near home plate where the batter stands

center: a football player who hands the ball to the quarterback to start a play

defense: the team that is trying to stop the other team from scoring during a football game

Division I: the top level of college football

draft: a yearly event in which teams take turns choosing new players from a group

field goals: kicks that go between the poles at the end of a football field. A field goal is worth three points.

foul: in basketball, a broken rule

Heisman Trophy: an award given each year to the most outstanding college football player

junior college: a school that students attend for two years after high school

linebacker: a defender who usually plays in the middle of the field

medical redshirt: a college athlete who doesn't play for one year due to injury

offense: the team that is trying to score during a football game

quarterback: a football player whose main job is to throw passes

running back: a football player whose main job is to run with the ball

safety: a defender whose main job is to prevent long passes

scouts: football experts who watch players to judge their abilities

snap: to start a football play by handing the ball to the quarterback

varsity: the top sports team at a school

wide receiver: a football player whose main job is to catch passes

Further Reading & Websites

Braun, Eric. *Super Football Infographics*. Minneapolis: Lerner Publications, 2015.

Kennedy, Mike, and Mark Stewart. *Touchdown: The Power and Precision of Football's Perfect Play*. Minneapolis: Millbrook Press, 2010.

Savage, Jeff. *Peyton Manning*. Minneapolis: Lerner Publications, 2013.

Cam Newton Foundation
https://www.cam1newton.com
Find out what the Cam Newton Foundation is doing at their official website.

The Official Site of the Carolina Panthers
http://www.panthers.com
The official website of the Panthers includes team schedules, news, profiles of past and present players and coaches, and much more.

Official Site of the National Football League
http://www.nfl.com
The NFL's official website provides fans with recent news stories, statistics, biographies of players and coaches, and information about games.

Sports Illustrated Kids
http://www.sikids.com
The *Sports Illustrated Kids* website covers all sports, including football.

LERNER
SOURCE

Expand learning beyond the printed book. Download free, complementary educational resources for this book from our website, www.lernersource.com.

Index

Photo Acknowledgments

The images in this book are used with the permission of: © Ezra Shaw/Getty Images, pp. 4, 5; © Michael Zagaris/Getty Images, p. 6; © Timothy A. Clark/AFP/Getty Images, p. 7; © Sean M. Haffey/Getty Images, p. 8; © Nickolay Khoroshkov/Shutterstock.com, p. 10; AP Photo/Jim Prisching, p. 11; Chris Szagola/Cal Sport Media/Newscom, p. 13; © Susan Stevenson/Shutterstock.com, p. 14; © Kim Klement/USA TODAY Sports, p. 17; © University of Florida/Collegiate Images/Getty Images, p. 18; Kenny Felt/ZumaPress.com/Newscom, pp. 20, 21; Shelby Daniels/Icon SMI/Newscom, p. 22; John Angelillo/UPI/Newscom, p. 23; AP Photo/Stephen Chemin, p. 24; AP Photo/David Kohl, p. 25; © Jeff Siner/Charlotte Observer/Getty Images, pp. 26, 28; AP Photo/Kent Smith, p. 29.

Front cover: John G. Mabanglo/Collection/Newscom.

Main body text set in Caecilia LT Std 55 Roman 16/28.
Typeface provided by Adobe Systems.